ESCAPE
FOR MOTHERS OF PRISONERS

ESCAPE
FOR MOTHERS OF PRISONERS

*An Uplifting Burst of Freedom
for a Mother's Soul*

GLORY S. DAVIS

Escape for Mothers of Prisoners

Copyright 2015 by Glory S. Davis
DavGlo Publishing, LLC
27372 Highway 21
Angie, Louisiana 70426

All rights reserved. No part of this publication may be reproduced, stored in a retrieval system, or transmitted, in any form or by any means, electronic, mechanical, photocopying or otherwise without the prior written permission of the publisher.

All scriptures marked HCSB are taken from the Holman Christian Standard Bible, copyright 1999, 2000, 2003, 2009, by Holman Bible Publishers. Used by permission.

All scriptures marked KJV are taken from King James Version of the Holy Bible.

Copyediting by Tyriah Davis
Cover and interior design by *wordzworth.com*

Library Congress Cataloging

ISBN (paperback) 978-0-9914475-4-1
ISBN (eBook) 978-0-9914475-5-8

Manufactured in the United States of America
First Edition

_____

Presented To

_____

Presented By

_____

Date

"And the peace of God, which passeth all understanding, shall keep your hearts and minds through Christ Jesus."

Philippians 4:7, KJV

This book is dedicated to my mother and father, Mr. and Mrs. Malinda S. and Terry Banks, who implanted within me a love for learning and the value of hard work. Without their solid foundation, this book would be impossible.

ACKNOWLEDGEMENTS

I am indebted to many relatives, friends, and acquaintances who gave me encouragement and professional opinions as I wrote *Escape for Mothers of Prisoners*.

I specifically thank my son, Thomas Davis, who gave me permission without objections to use our personal story in this book. I thank Rhonda Peters, author of *So, What Can I Eat Now, and* Lubertha Peters who gave me useful suggestions and encouragement in all stages of the book's development. Also, I thank Tyriah G. Davis for copyediting and Kenyardy Jefferson, Emma Ross, Glory Brown, and Shelly Babers for their much needed support.

Finally, I thank God for the inspiration and spiritual guidance given to me as I pondered ideas, for the stamina and determination that were necessary to complete the project, and for the assurance that *Escape for Mothers of Prisoners* is a worthwhile endeavor that will benefit many mothers.

CONTENTS

Preface	ii
Escape Waits for the Righteous	1
Thoughts	3
Trust God	4
Truth – Behavior Comes from the Heart	6
Fear is a Snare	9
Love the Scorner	11
Get Control	16
Don't Cry	18
Jesus Will Cry with Us	19
Jesus Will Never Cast You Off	23
He's Always There	25
Have an Understanding Heart	26
Change Your Messages	28
Re-direct	30
Believe in Jesus / Avoid the Shame	33
Remain Faithful No Matter What	36
Forgive and Be Forgiven	39
In All Sincerity Confess	41
Guard the Peace	44
Peace	47
Go a Second Mile and More	49
A Mother's Part	52
Restore – But Withhold Support of Destructive Behaviors	53
Behold Thy Mother	56
Afterword	57
About the Author	59

PREFACE

My husband died May 10, in 1999 two weeks before our son's graduation from high school. I had no serious problems with my son until a month later when he told me that in two weeks he didn't have to follow any of my directions. By law, he was correct; for, he was turning 18 years old. Legally, I could not make him do anything. I thought that he was just hurting, grieving over his father's death, and he would soon get over it. I was wrong. He began a downward spiral that led from juvenile court and community service to a seven year stint in the Louisiana State Penitentiary as a multiple offender for drugs distribution.

I was devastated, and I could not understand how I found myself in such a situation. Crying, I sat in my room on the day that my son was sentenced, turning back time sorting through events in our lives trying to make sense of it all. Why had it happened? We were good people. What did I do wrong? Why didn't I see it coming?

Helplessness, shame, anger, fear, worry, self-blame, hate, loneliness, isolation: all kind of emotions and all kinds of thoughts pledged me that horrible day that my son was sentenced. When the doors were shut on my son, I, too, was imprisoned. Though I was home going to work and to church as usual, my isolation, was just as real as any prisoner. I knew that I needed help – to escape. But where could I turn for comfort, for counseling, for understanding? In my small village, when someone dies in your family, the whole community comes offering, food, money, comfort;

but, when a son or daughter goes off to prison, no one – not even friends – comes to offer support.

With no money for counseling, overtime, I turned to my Bible for strength, peace, comfort, and … ESCAPE that I could not find elsewhere. Gradually, healing came, and I slipped outside of myself to offer hope to other mothers of prisoners that I could not find in friends or other literature for myself. With love and understanding, I have written *Escape for Mothers of Prisoners,* a self-help book of meditations written especially for you who may be experiencing imprisonment because of a child's incarceration.

The scriptures used in this book are quoted from the King James Version of the Holy Bible (KJV) or the Holman Christian Standard Bible (HCSB), the digital text.

Finally, may you renew your relationship with God and find comfort and freedom for your soul as you escape your own personal prison by meditating on the emotions or concerns, common with mothers of prisoners, covered in this book.

"Christ has liberated us to be free. Stand firm then and don't submit again to a yoke of slavery."

GALATIANS 5: 1 HCSB.

When you feel like a prisoner, read…

ESCAPE WAITS FOR THE RIGHTEOUS

"Be assured that the wicked will not go unpunished, but the offspring of the righteous will escape."

Proverbs 11:21 HCSB

If you feel like a prisoner because your child is in prison, you are not alone. I for one feel the same way. May be it is because of all the demands – the need for clothing and hygiene supplies, the visitation time and expense, the collect phone calls, the fees, the stringent rules and regulations – that the Child's prison burdens the parents with. On the other hand, maybe it is the maternal bond that all mothers have with their children which binds them as one and makes them feel that they too are in prison. Whatever the reason is one thing is sure: whenever a child goes to prison, the mother feels like a prisoner and need some means to escape. But, where can she find escape from the tremendous demands put her because of her new found title – mother of a prisoner?

First, before you can fine escape, you must achieve inner peace. And, the best way to do that is to learn to be content in the state you are in. Accept the reality of your child imprisonment and learn to cope with it. Next, try meditating. It helps to rank your values, to relieve tension, and to clear your mind of negativity. Also, make it a regular practice of reading the Bible. You will be surprise of the inner peace that comes from concentrating on things spiritual and connecting to a higher power.

Second, between the collect calls, the visitations, and requests for money, schedule some "me time" in which you do only those things that give you pleasure. Some good ideas are taking in a movie, going for a walk, or going shopping. For me, a thing like shopping increases my endorphins and not only helps me to escape and destress but also helps me to relieve pain. In a way, a temporary detour from the pressures of life reenergizes me and gives me strength to continue when I do return. Third, as soon as possible, learn the prison system in which your child is confined. Find out as much as you can about the rules and regulations and the dress code for visitors. Doing so will save you time, money, and frustration. I shall never forget the time that I drove three hours for a visit only to find that I was improperly dressed in sandals. Imagine my frustration as I searched for a store to buy shoes and to return for the visit before it was too late – something I could have avoided by researching beforehand.

Fourth and finally, step outside of self and extend a helping hand to those in need. In other words, volunteer. Volunteering helps us to escape self, and it rewards us far more than the gifts we give. Also, remember these words from Proverbs 11: 21: the wicked will not go unpunished, but the offspring of the righteous will escape. The implication of this verse for mothers is that if we remain children righteous and faithful to Christ, there is both escape and life waiting for us just around the corner.

Heavenly Father, behold us mothers of prisoner, bless us with a peace of mind that will allow us to escape the pressures of coping with the prison system, and give us the freedom we need in order to enjoy life. In Jesus' name, we pray.

THOUGHTS

Not all prisons are brick and mortar.
Some are ghost, self-imposed,
That creep into the mind
And haunt the very soul.

A child may never see
The halo around your head.
A child may never know
That he is loved so.

There comes a time indeed
When a mother must see the need
And escape the bars that bind
In search of peace of mind.

A woman's joy flows freely
Bringing smiles to one and all.
A women's sorrow sways sadly
When a loved one slips and falls.

When you feel helpless, read…

TRUST GOD

"I can do all things through Christ which strengthens me."

PHILIPPIANS 4: 13 KJV

One of the hardest things for a mother to endure is to see her child in shackles bound like a vicious animal and locked away for five, ten, or maybe twenty years. For her, helplessness is the order of day. She feels that her back is against the wall, that all of her enemies are closing in on her, and that she has nothing with which to defend herself or her child.

If, by chance, you find yourself the mother of a prisoner and feeling helpless, consider drawing strength from our Lord and Savior, Jesus Christ. He, unlike lawyers who will sometime give you a sloppy defense or friends who may leave you without offering aid or comfort, will give you the power needed to stand strong at such a difficult time in your life. He has said that His strength in made perfect in our weakness (2 Corinthians: 13). The implication for us is that when we are helpless, God's grace and power increase and bring us victory.

Mothers, we will also do well to draw strength from the lives of our biblical ancestors, too. Take David for an example. He faced and defeated a giant, Goliath, who had threatened and frightened many of his people. How did he do it? With only a stone and a sling shot, he relied on God to give him the strength that he needed for victory (1 Samuel 17). God delivered David, and He will deliver you too. There is no need to feel helpless. Trust God.

Heavenly Father, when we are powerless,
give us the strength that we need to stand strong
against the Goliaths in our lives. Help us
learn contentment and patience as we wait for your
victory and the return of our loved ones.
In Jesus' name, we pray. Amen.

When you are helpless down and out
And your hope is all but gone,
Find heavenly comfort and perfect peace
By putting your trust in God alone.

When you feel guilty, read…

TRUTH – BEHAVIOR COMES FROM THE HEART

"For when the Gentiles, which have not the law, do by nature the things contained in the law, these, having not the law, are a law unto themselves: Which shows the work of the law written in their hearts, their conscience also bearing witness…"

ROMANS 2: 14-15 KJV

Mothers are reflective creatures who tend to look back and analyze situations to find meanings or reasons why. When their children are in trouble or are sentenced to confinement, they are quick to blame themselves. All kinds of questions haunt them. What did I do wrong? What could I have done better? These are just two of the many worries that bother mothers as they replay the events of their child's problem. The truth is many mothers are free of guilt; for the child's behavior comes from within and is ultimately beyond the mother's control.

By nature we are all endowed from birth with a conscience, a little voice that leads us to reject or accept the will of God (Romans 2:14-15a). Each day we make thousands of choices deciding whether to choose good or bad. What amazes me most is that the choice to do "good" or to live holy can be made prior to any knowledge of the law – or right and wrong.

Consider Father Abraham's choices for examples. Long before God gave Moses the law, Abraham walked upright with God and was a perfect model of God's goodness. How did he do it? How could he know what was right if he had never been taught right and wrong? The answer lies in Romans 2: 14-15. The work of the law was written in his heart. The implication for us is that the desire and the choice to do good come from within from the heart – even without the mother's instructions. Similarly, the desire to choose "bad" can comes from the child's heart in spite of the mother's instructions.

As mothers we have the job "to train a child in way he should go" (Proverbs 22:6). Most good mothers do just that. But we must remember we can lead a cow to the water, but we can't make him drink. In the end, it is the cow that must lean over the pond and take a drink himself. By the same token, we can teach a child right and wrong; we can even model it for him. But that is as far as it goes. In the end it is the child with the help of his conscience or inner voice who chooses to cling to our teachings or to reject them. When the child rejects the sound instructions of his parents and ends in prison, who is guilty, the parent or the child? Of course, it is the child! We don't blame the farmer when the cow doesn't drink. Don't blame yourself when your child chooses not to accept your instructions.

> *Loving Father, help us to understand that the desire to choose right or wrong can come from the heart of the child before and sometimes in spite of instructions from his parents. When we have dedicated all energies to molding good children, and they reject our instructions, remove all guilt from us and help us to remain steadfast in confidence that one day they will do like the prodigal son and come to themselves. In Jesus' name, we pray. Amen.*

When you are afraid read…

FEAR IS A SNARE

*"The fear of a man is a snare,
but the one who trust in the Lord is protected."*

PROVERBS 29:25 HCSB

Fear plagues a mother when her child is in prison. She sees it in her child's eyes and hears it in his or her voice even though the child tries to conceal it from her. She is afraid that someone will hurt her child, that he or she will be too cold, too hungry, or too hot. The truth is fear is dangerous and hinders one's actions in all areas.

Fear is a dangerous snare because it is very harmful to one's health. How? In its worst form it causes stress which is one of the root causes of many harmful ailments, including heart trouble, diabetes, high blood pressure, depression, digestive problems, sleep problems and autoimmune diseases. In addition, it causes an inability to concentrate and poor judgment. Fear is also bad because it hinders action. How? Because we are afraid of the negative consequences from an encounter, we avoid that encounter. That means that if you are afraid to confront lawyers or judges about your child's case, you will probably avoid them. In the long run, you are rendered ineffective in helping. No wonder Proverbs calls fear a snare!

What is the answer to this dangerous emotion? The best answer lies in the Lord who has promised protection. Proverbs 4: 25-26 informs us not to fear danger of ruin of the wicked; for the Lord will keep your foot from a snare. The implication for us is that we have no need to fear anyone. Why? The Lord who is all powerful will shield us from any danger. Turn to Him first and meditate on his scriptures. Some that will bring you comfort and strength are 1 John 4: 18, Palms 23: 4-5, Palms 27: 1-3, and 2 Timothy 1:7.

 Dear Lord, when we face fear, stand with us and give us the courage that we need to confront our enemies or any life defining issues that may threaten us. Turn our fear into love for you and for others. In Jesus' name, we pray. Amen.

When you feel scorn, read…

LOVE THE SCORNER

"But I say unto to you, Love your enemies, bless them that curse you, do good to them that hate you, and pray for them which despitefully use you, and persecute you."

MATTHEW 5: 44 KJV

Mothers are angels sent from God entrusted with the care of His children. They have been given special qualities such as love, understanding, kindness, and care to guarantee that they do an excellent job. When their children are successful, they are called good mothers, but when their children are not, mothers are often ridiculed and scorned.

When my child was sentenced to jail, he literally lost his name. Instead of being called by his name, he was referred to as Mrs. Davis's child. I felt that I was defined by my child's actions and ridiculed through the persuasive technique called association. Calling me the mother of a troublesome child was saying to the world that I too was bad. Don't get me wrong. I am not saying that I wanted to disassociate from my child. What I am saying is that we mothers should be recognized because of our accomplishments – not by our children's short comings or personal achievements. Too often, doing so will present an eschewed picture of the child or of the mother.

People often mask their shortcoming by ridiculing some fault in others. Really, if we uncover the mask of those who belittle us, we will find that they are hurting and have many more problems than we ever had. Because this is true, we should always take the higher road. What do I mean by that? Instead of fighting back or degrading ourselves by retaliating with sarcastic remarks, we should pray for those who seem to find pleasure in pointing out our faults. In other words, love the scorner.

What good is there in praying for enemies or loving the scorner? Praying for those who spitefully use you reflects that you understand their masked feeling and that you love them. Moreover, when you love your enemies, you prove your love for God and show the world a view of God's perfect love which rains on both the just and the unjust. In the end, because you love those who hate you, you are rewarded greatly.

Heavenly Father give us the strength to ignore the scorn and ridicule of others. Help us to always take the higher road and love both our friends and our enemies so that we may be a living example of your perfect love to the world. In Jesus' name, we pray. Amen.

KARMA

When you're a victim of scorner's hate,
Because of what your child has done,
Hold your head high and don't you frown
Nor stoop to low levels on the ground.

Pray for your enemies and all of those
Who dare point you out in hate.
Rest assured that they may feel
What you feel some later date.

RISE, SHINE, GLORIFY GOD

Rise, a new day is dawning.
No time to sleep;
Before that great getting up morning,
There are appointments to keep.

Oh get up! Get up! I said.
The Master is on His way.
Signs blink clear ahead
Announcing the final judgment day.

Shine, you represent the Savior.
Put on your best attires.
Shed all that bad behavior
And do what the Lord requires.

Set your light upon a hill
So all the world can see
Our Lord and Savior's will
Shinning for Him and me.

Abide in Christ with all your heart.
Glorify, oh glorify Him each day.
Live life fully but set apart
From Satan and evil in every way.

Refrain from anger and forsake wraft. Fret not yourself; it tends only to evil."

PSALMS 37:8 KJV

"Good sense makes one slow to anger, and it is his glory to overlook an offense."

PROVERB 19:11 KJV

"Know this, my beloved brothers: let every person be quick to hear, slow to speak, slow to anger; for the anger of man does not produce the righteousness of God."

JAMES 1: 19-20 KJV

When you feel anger, read…

GET CONTROL

*"Refrain from anger and give up rage;
do not be agitated – it can only bring harm."*

PSALM 37: 8 HCSB

Mothers –like hens that will attack anyone who disturbs their chicks –are very protective of their children. When a mother feels that her child is in harm's way, in anger she fights back, attacking the enemy or anyone whom she thinks may be sided with the enemy. If your child has had several run-ins with the law, then no doubt you have harbored anger against the law, against your child's co-defendants, or against the system as a whole. In some cases, you may even be angry with your child. If you are not careful, anger can be very destructive to you, to innocent people, or to the object of your anger.

How can anger be destructive, you might ask? First consider the dangers it may cause to your health. High blood pressure, heart attack, strokes, headaches, depression, and anxiety are just a few of the problems caused by the stress of anger. This may seem a little far-fetched, but with heart attacks and strokes in the list, anger can literally kill you. Second, anger can destroy careers and relationships. How? Often anger is redirected toward innocent people. Both children and spouses may suffer because of some unresolved anger linked to a person's past. Jobs may be lost because of an angry person's inability to work well with people. Third, extreme anger can cause a person to argue, fight, or even kill. How many cases can you cite in which a person killed a friend, a spouse, or a loved one during a fit of rage?

Since anger is so dangerous, it is advisable that you take means to control it. But How? Rather than isolate yourself when your child is in prison, get involved in activities that require you to do some physical exercise. Walking, running, playing sports, and fishing are a few activities that may be effective. For, they are known to reduce stress, an underlining cause of anger. Also, consider reading more meditations. They provide counseling, aid judgment, change attitude, and give you the peace of mind needed in calming anger. Last and most important, seek help from God. Reading the Bible, going to church, communing with others, and praying will renew your outlook and rekindle your love for others.

As Christians we must remember that God is our protector, and He has our best interest at heart at all times. We have no need to argue or fight; He will protect us. If we take matters into our own hands, we show a lack of faith in God. Heaven forbid! On the other hand, if we trust God to solve our problems and wait for his solution, life is better for us and all involved. What is more, we just may win our enemy as a friend.

Heavenly Father, help us to understand that anger is just as destructive to us as it is to the object of our anger. Increase our faith in you so that we may freely trust you to solve all our disputes in our favor. In Jesus' name, we pray. Amen.

REVELATION 21: 4

DON'T CRY

*Don't Cry
Mother, don't you dare cry.
God sees your teary eye.
If you pray to Him today,
He'll wash your pain away.*

When feeling the need for sympathy, read…

JESUS WILL CRY WITH US

"For we do not have a high priest who is unable to sympathize with our weaknesses, but One who has been tested in every way as we are, yet without sin. Therefore let us approach the throne of grace with boldness, so that we may receive mercy and find grace to help us at the proper time."

HEBREWS 4:15-16 HSCB

Mothers are a bundle of emotions. Because they are, they display love, joy, pride, and a host of other positive feelings. Though mothers often turn these emotions toward others, they have a need to feel them themselves coming from others. Take sympathy for an example. Mothers are very sympathetic people, and they show others that they care all the time. However, mothers need to feel compassion and want friends and acquaintances to empathize with their plight as well. When someone says to them, I understand, I get it, or I feel your pain, mothers get encouragement that allows them to endure that pain.

When mothers of prisoners need encouragement or renewed hope for the good will of their children, they should be careful to avoid negative people. Why? They are like the friends who came to comfort Job –poor comforters. Instead of being supportive, Job's friends accused him of some secret sin for which he needed to confess. Rather than give him encouragement, they made him confused and sometime doubtful (Book of Job). Job would have been better off without such friends. Also, negative people are contagious. They tend to spread their negativity on people who are vulnerable. Mothers, who are facing opposition from the authorities and who are opened to attack, may very well become negative themselves.

Rather than keep company with negative people, mothers, turn to Jesus for support. In Hebrews 4: 15-16, we read that He is able to sympathize with our weakness. Why? He has been tested in every way that we have and He is able to extend mercy and grace to help us at a time in our lives when we are in dire need of it.

In other words, Jesus will sympathize and cry with us. Just think! Jesus cried with Mary and others when they were sad over Lazarus's death and raised him. (John 11:35). What is to keep him from giving us sympathy and help when our love ones are in trouble?

Christ our Lord, help us to remember that you were once fully human and fully capable of feeling our pain. Today, when we hurt, hurt with us; when we cry, cry with us. And, when we need your grace and mercy, rain them down on us. In your holy name, we pray. Amen.

"Haven't I commanded you: Be courageous? Do not be afraid or discouraged, for the Lord your God is with you wherever you go."

JOSHUA 1:9

"When thou passest through the waters, I will be with thee, and through the rivers, they will not overflow thee: when thou walkest through fire, thou shall not be burned; neither shall the flame kindle upon thee."

ISAIAH 43:2

When you feel abandoned, read…

JESUS WILL NEVER CAST YOU OFF

*"For the Lord will not cast off his people,
neither will he forsake his inheritance."*

PSALM 94:14, KJV

*L*ittle children crying, *"They want play with me,"* grownups striving to become members of secret clubs, and teenagers trying-out for cheerleaders, football, or track: all have something in common – a need to belong. Every one of us has an inborn need to belong or to be accepted by others. Mothers are no different. They long to be loved by their friends, children, or close relatives.

When they feel rejected by their friends, mothers suffer a blow to their emotional well-being. But, when they feel rejected, as they so often are, by their friends because of their children's mistakes, the blow can be almost devastating.

What is a mother to do when she thinks that her friends have separated from her because of her children? Should she blame others? No, her feeling of abandonment may be a personal reaction to the separation from her child who is in prison. Because of her hurt over that separation, she may have only fantasized that others were distancing themselves from her, too. When in actuality, she is the one who distanced herself from others.

If you are a mother with abandonment issues, be sure to find the real cause for your feelings and treat that cause. One good way to find peace of mind is to seek counseling or join a support group that may understand your feelings and may be able to offer workable solutions. However, the best way to find relief from feelings of abandonment is to seek the comfort of our Lord and Savior Jesus Christ. Psalms 94:14 informs us that he will not cast off his people. Both his Word and His examples can bring us peace. Through His Word, we learn that we are never alone if we are in a relationship with Him. For, He has promised to never leave us or forsake us. From His example we learn that when we are right, we need not seek revenge from the ones who desert or separate from us. God will make things right for us. Consider what happened to Judas and Peter when they abandoned Jesus for examples –one wept bitterly in sorrow, and the other hang himself (Luke: 22:62; Matthew 27:5).

Heavenly Father, help us to understand that you, unlike friends who may forsake us or who may separate from us, will never leave us alone. Increase our faith in you so that we may always feel your presence no matter where or how we are. In Jesus' name, we pray. Amen.

HE'S ALWAYS THERE

*If you seek someone to care
Try Jesus; He's always there.*

*He's a doctor, nurse, and lawyer too
And will counsel you on what to do.*

*If you give Him all your heart,
He will surely do His Part.*

*Unlike a friend who slips away.
Jesus will stay from day to day.*

When You Feel Disrespected, read…

HAVE AN UNDERSTANDING HEART

"The Lord is close to the brokenhearted, and he saves those whose spirits have been crushed."

Psalm 34:18 HCSB

"You're not the boss of me" is a declaration that I have heard often from a small child being corrected by a sibling. My neighbor's children and my students have even shouted these words at me when I attempted to discipline them. However, never in my wildest dreams did I think that I would hear this statement or one like it from my child. Unfortunately, I did, and it left me feeling disrespected and brokenhearted.

What is a mother to do when the child that she fed, nursed, protected, and guided for 17 or 18 years turns on her and declares that he does not have to follow her directions?

The first impulse is to let the child hit a brick wall and suffer the consequences. However, thank goodness that is not the last thought. Hopefully, after the shock of such a statement, you will do all that you can to prevent your child from destroying himself. That's what good mothers do. Perhaps you should reread the story of the "Prodigal Son" (Luke 15: 11-31). In it, the youngest son, showing rebellion and disrespect for his father, asks for his inheritance and leaves. He squanders his fortune and consequently finds himself eating with pigs. When he comes to himself, he goes back home to his father. Guess what? The father is overjoyed to see him and gives a celebration in his honor. That is what God does when one of His Children go astray and return; that is what we should do, too, when our children rebel against us and later return.

Since outward rebellion usually has underlying problems as its cause, try to find and understand the root of your child's show of disrespect. It may not concern you at all. It could be that you were a convenient punching bag at the time. What you should do is to have an understanding heart and give all the support that you can. By no means should you follow his example and desert him. Love your child even though he may be unlovable.

How can we return disrespect with love when we are brokenhearted, and poor in spirit? Easily. Psalms 34:18 informs us that the Lord is close to the brokenhearted and he save those whose spirits has been crushed. Put your trust in the Lord and rely on Him for strength. He will heal your broken heartedness and solve your child's problem as well.

 Heavenly Father, help us to stand strong in the face of our children's rebellion and disrespect. Remove from us the desire to retaliate and give us an understanding, supportive heart. In Jesus' name, we pray. Amen.

When you feel the need
for contentment, read…

CHANGE YOUR MESSAGES

"Not that I speak in respect of want; for I have learned, in whatsoever state I am, therewith to be content."

PHILIPPIANS 4: 11, KJV

Have you ever experienced a situation in your life in which you could not find satisfaction no matter where you looked? Have you ever noticed that your favorite foods didn't taste the same anymore, that the people you once enjoyed were not fun anymore; or that the things that you once loved doing no longer held your attention? Have you ever been restless and depressed at the same time? If you have experienced any of these, then you can imagine the discontentment I felt because of the imprisonment of my son.

How did I snap out of that pitiful state? I worked to change the messages that I sent to myself. Instead of telling myself that I could not get satisfaction, I told myself that I was content and happy with my life. To help me reinforce that message, I copied Philippians 4:11 and posted it on my desk, on the refrigerator, and in other conspicuous places. Every time that I noticed that scripture, I repeated it silently. In addition, whenever I got an idea that something didn't taste right or didn't look right or that I didn't feel right, I change that thought to its opposite. My self-talk worked, and gradually I changed my outlook.

Because I believe that the Bible has solutions for all of man's problems, I added the regular reading of it and meditating on it to my practice of positive self-talk. What good did it do? It reassured me that through God I have freedom from fear or anxiety. Moreover, each time I prayed and felt the benefits of God's grace and mercy, my faith and hope increased – sending me to a better state.

 Dear God, help us to understand that the best way to cure discontentment is to change our way of thinking. Draw us closer to you, shower us with your grace and mercy, and give us the assurance we need to live happy, satisfied lives. In Jesus' name, we pray. Amen.

When you feel grief on holidays and birthdays, read...

RE-DIRECT

"...Brethren, whatsoever things are true, whatsoever things are honest, whatsoever things are just, whatsoever things are pure, whatsoever things are lovely, whatsoever things are of good report; if there be any virtue, and if there be any praise, think on these things."

PHILIPPIANS 4: 8 KJV

Tinnitus is a condition characterized by a constant ringing in the ear. There is little or no cure for it. Consequently, sufferers are at its mercy, and the ringing continues in their ears sometimes for years. Some doctors prescribe a white noise machine not as a cure for the ringing but as a means to divert the sufferer's attention from the noise. In a way, tinnitus sufferers and grieving mothers of prisoners have at least two things in common.

Both the condition and the treatment are similar for each. Like the constant ringing in the ear of tinnitus sufferers, the holiday and birthday grieving never stops for mothers of prisoners. And the pain seems to get worse with time. In addition, for treatment, both grieving mothers and tinnitus sufferers benefit from a means of diversion.

Tinnitus sufferers use a white noise machine to divert their attention from the noise. Likewise, mothers of prisoners can engage in a series of refreshing activities which will – like a noise machine- draw their attention away from their depressing problems.

Here are a few good suggestions that are sure to help the grieving mothers snap back from their misery: First, invest in volunteering. It is sure to return positive dividends and make you feel good about yourself for a change. Second, initiate a service project to benefit the poor. A good idea may be a project collecting donations for prisoners without family support. Third, have a good laugh. Not to yourself, but go to the movies with a BFF and see a good comedy …or read a funny book. The laugh will lift your soul and de-stress you in the process. Fourth, go on a treasure hunt to antique shops, thrift shops, or garage sales. It is amazing how some of the items in these unconventional shopping places pull you back into history and draw you away from your problem. Fifth, do something special for yourself. For example, buy that dress or those shoes that you have adored but denied yourself for long time. Believe it or not, each of these activities and other like them will re-direct you from the road to depression and put you on a better road to happiness instead.

In summary, remember Paul's advice from Philippians 4:8. Think or focus your energies only on good things – those grounded in the teachings and will of Jesus Christ. If you do, you will always have a positive outlook on life and your depressive attitude will become a thing of the past.

Heavenly Father, we thank you for the inspiration of this message. May it be beneficial to all mothers grieving in the absence of their children? Help us mothers to keep our mind stayed on those things that are just, pure, honest, and good; so that, we may enjoy your peace and rid ourselves of grief forever. In Jesus' name, we pray. Amen.

When you feel ashamed, read...

BELIEVE IN JESUS / AVOID THE SHAME

"Now the scripture says, Everyone who believes on Him will not be put to shame."

ROMANS 10:11 HCSB

I am almost ashamed to say it, but when my son was sentenced to prison, I was humiliated, embarrassed, and just plain ashamed. Why? I had sponsored drug awareness programs in my community, had taught drug awareness in the school and in the church, and had pulled boys aside and warned them about the dangers of drugs. Yet, in my self-righteousness, I had not recognized the misuse of drugs in my own son. I thought that I was the laughing stock of the town and found it hard to hold my head up.

If you are feeling ashamed because of your son's imprisonment, I want you to know that you are not alone. Shame is a common emotion with mothers of prisoners. But, it need not be, especially if you have done everything in your power to give your child the very best opportunities. Once you face reality and admit to yourself and others that your child is in lock up, healing can began and the shame wills gradually fade.

To stop the gossip among the neighbors, talk freely about your son's situation. Tell them as much as you can about his case without causing harm to it. Put it out in the open is what I say. If you do, people will have nothing to gossip about. And what is more, it will be as therapeutic to you as addressing Alcoholic Anonymous is for the alcoholic. Nine times out of ten, people will empathize with your situation, and you will find – as I did –that your shame is the results of the standards that you hold for yourself – not because of what others have done or said to you.

Since our shame may be because of the attitude and values that we have acquired for ourselves, then it might be good to do a little prioritizing. We need to ask ourselves which is most important— my relationship with my child or my public image? By all means we should swallow our pride, choose our child, and support him or her no matter what. Our children should always be placed before our public image.

From a religious viewpoint, consider Romans 10: 3. In it we read, "For they being ignorant of God's righteousness, and going about to establish their own righteousness, have not submitted themselves unto the righteousness of God". The implication for us is that when we fail to recognize God and His Might, we may set ourselves up as righteous and all powerful. Doing so will give us a feeling of pride that may easily be subject to shame. However, if we recognize the righteousness of God, we will see how small we are in comparison. Focusing on God will eliminate our pride and consequently any likelihood of shame. For the bottom line, we can safely say then that there is no shame for those who believe in Christ Jesus- neither here or in the hereafter.

Our Lord and Savior Jesus Christ, when we feel shame, help us to stay focused on you – for your example of one who endured shame for the greater good… and for your power and might which help us to live humbly before you. In Jesus' name, we pray. Amen.

When you doubt God, read…

REMAIN FAITHFUL NO MATTER WHAT

"But let him ask in faith without doubting. For the doubter is like the surging sea, driven and tossed by the wind."

JAMES 1:6 HCSB

We mothers, like everybody when they are having trouble or hardships, question God. We usually want to know why. Why did such misfortune come to me, we ask daily in prayers? When we can't get a reasonable answer, we doubt whether God even exist. Are we sinning when we doubt? No. Is doubting God dangerous? Yes, when we doubt God we become opened to the attacks from the devil, and we may very well be persuaded by any imposter or cult that comes along.

When we have doubts because of hardships, pain and trouble, we should be like Job, from the Book of Job, and remain faithful to God no matter what. Job lost his beloved sons, daughters, servants, and all his possessions. But, when his wife told him to curse God and die, he insisted that she speaks like a foolish women (Job 2:10). He later declared to his comforters, though he slays me yet will I trust Him; but I will remain mine own before him (Job 13: 15). Job remained steadfast in his faith in God even though his skin was stricken with boils. In the end, because of his faithfulness, Job was restored exponentially.

The lesson that we draw from Job's story is that if we remain faithful to God at all times – even when our prayers are seemingly unanswered, He will not desert us, nor will He let us be destroyed. In the end, he will reward us for our faithfulness. But, how can we remain faithful when our prayers are seemingly not answered, you may ask? The keys are trust and patience. We must trust that God works in our favor even during bad times, and we must wait patiently for Him to restore us.

 Dear God, when we doubt, shield us form the attacks of the devil that are sure to come and help us to faithfully wait for your mercy and grace at all times. In Jesus' name, we pray. Amen.

Crucifixion of Jesus
Print from St. Michaels Cathedral by Michael van Coxie

"Then said Jesus, Father forgive them for they know not what that they do. And they parted his raiments and cast lots."

LUKE 23:34 KJV

When you can't forgive, read…

FORGIVE AND BE FORGIVEN

"For if you forgive men their trespasses, your father will also forgive you. But, if you forgive not men their trespasses, neither will your father forgive you."

MATTHEWS 6: 14-15 KJV

*I*s it easy for a mother to forgive? No, however it is in her best interest if she can forgive. Why? If she can forgive those who trespasses against her, God and others will forgive her. But, if she withholds her forgiveness, she endangers her health, her safety, and her chances to enter the kingdom.

How does not forgiving others endanger your health and safety? Research suggests that it increases anxiety, stress, and depression. We all know that those demons can take their toll on the heart and nerves. It is not rare that stress and depression can lead to murder or suicide.

Remember what happened to many disgruntled workers who stormed their former work sights and killed others and themselves to get even. Specifically, take for example Mark Essex who killed 9 people and was killed himself because of a rage motivated by racism. So really, when we fail to forgive, we fail to guard our own health and safety.

How does not forgiving others endanger your chance to enter the kingdom? First, it closes the door to God's forgiveness to you. Consider what happened to the unforgiving debtor in Matthew 18: 23-35 for an example. A servant owed the king a large sum of money but had none. When the king threatens to sell the servant's family and possessions, the servant asks for forgiveness and receives it. Later, the servant, himself, is owed a small sum of money. When his debtor fails to pay him, the servant seizes the debtor and throws him in prison. When the king hears of his servant lack of compassion, he condemns the servant to the tormentors in prison. God has no tolerance with his servants who will not forgive others is the lesson. He will surly punish them. For He said in Romans 12: 19 "vengeance is mine, I will repay." Let Him.

Heavenly Father, help us to learn from the example of your darling son Jesus who was able to say "father forgive them" even while he hung from the cross. Rid us of bitterness before it destroys our health and condemns us to hell. In Jesus' name, we pray.
Amen.

When you feel the need to confess, read…

IN ALL SINCERITY CONFESS

"The one who conceals his sins will not prosper, but whoever confesses and renounces them will find mercy."

PROVERBS 28:13 HCSB

A student of mine was constantly in trouble, either with another student, her parents, or the law. Her attitude was worse than any I had ever witness, and every fourth word out of her mouth was barroom profanity. She did not respect me, the other students, or the principal, and she was constantly fighting. The only peaceful day I had at school that year occurred when she was absent.

When I checked the home situation, I learned that the student had watched her father kill her mother. In shock, she had remained quiet when her father told the policemen that she -not he- was the murderer. Sadly, she stayed months in juvenile custody before the truth was discovered, and the judge sent her back to public school. By that time though, her behavior had changed from mild manner to almost incorrigible.

What do we learn from that story? Many times a child's bad behavior manifests itself because of abuse, neglect, or poor parenting. And, sometimes, like in the case with this student, abused children fail to adjust in school and in society. Because of the trauma of suppressed emotions from bad situations, these children later find themselves in jail – guilty by reasons of poor parenting.

When a mother recognizes that she is responsible for her child's bad behavior or imprisonment because of poor parenting or some means, what should she do? Should she seek forgiveness from her child and takes steps to correct what she has done? Should she seek counseling for herself so that she may avoid making the same mistake again? Or, should she confess her sins to God and ask for His mercy? Really, a guilty mother who has destroyed her child's life, should do all of the above. She should by no means conceal her shortcoming. In all sincerity, she should make confession to God and make things right with her child.

Proverbs 28:13 tells us that the one who conceals sin will not proper, but whoever confesses and renounces it will find mercy. The implication is: all mothers who are burden by a wrong done to their children is that they can find escape from that wrong by confessing and renouncing it before God. He has promised to give us mercy if we do so.

Heavenly Father, we thank you for entrusting us with the care of your children. Help us to do the very best for them always. If we error and lead them astray, have mercy on us and give us the desire and the wisdom to make things right. In Jesus' name, we pray. Amen.

"If we confess our sins, he is faithful and just to forgive us our sins, and to cleanse us from all unrighteousness."

1 JOHN 1:9

When you feel the need for unity in the family, read…

GUARD THE PEACE

"And Jesus knew their thoughts and said unto them, 'Every kingdom divided against itself is brought to desolation; and every city or house divided against itself shall not stand.'"

MATTHEW 12: 25 KJV

When a child steps outside the circle of a good family's beliefs or values system and does something that is uncharacteristic of that family – like sells drugs, steals, or kills someone, – he causes confusion and disunity that is not easily solved. Why? Because his problem or imprisonment causes a huge financial burden that robs from the other children's welfare, and because his problem may steals all of the mother's attention away from those children, hardship, fighting, and jealousy may rear their heads. If this happens, a mother finds herself in the middle of chaos. Not only must she fight to survive a system that has claimed one of her children, but she also has to fight to mend a relationship with her other children who have alienated themselves from her. To put it simply, mothers of prisoners may find themselves fighting two wars – one outside of the house with the system and one inside of the house with a family divided.

Take my situation for an example. I have two sons. When one son got in trouble, the cost of bail and lawyers exploded my already tight budget. I had to decide which took priority – my son in trouble or the one who was doing well. I chose to go after the lost sheep and put all my energies and money in helping the one with the problems. After all, he needed me the most at that time. My decision was not accepted by my other son. He accused me of favoritism and isolated himself from me. I recognized his behavior as jealousy and admit that the war with that son and his separation from me was the hardest to bear. Why? I felt that I had made the right decision and was broken-hearted because I was misunderstood.

That brings me to the question: what is a mother to do when her decisions or actions cause division in the family? How can she knit the family back together again when it has been torn by jealousy? The answers to these questions are not easy, but here are some suggestions. First, examine your actions and decisions and make sure that you have done the right thing. If you have done something wrong, admit it and ask for forgiveness. Second, explain the reasons for your decision to the alienated child and solicit his or her understanding. In my case, I told my son that I treated each of them as individuals and that I would do the same for him if he needed it. If you don't get support from that child, don't press or argue; give him or her time to heal. Third, even though the child may be angry with you, be kind to him or her in spite of the behavior. When the time is right, arrange family visits with the one in prison and spend some quality time with the alienated child alone, making sure to do all you can to restore unity.

Lastly, remember these words from Matthew 12: 25: "a house divided against itself cannot stand." It is your responsibility as a mother to maintain unity between each of you. Whenever one of your children is in need, do whatever you can to help, and if other problems, such as jealousy, complicate matters, it is also your responsibility to guard peace and maintain unity. Good luck!

Heavenly father, when we are faced with confusion and division in our homes, give us the foresight of Isaiah, the wisdom of Solomon, and the compassion of your darling son Jesus. Help us to use these qualities collectively to restore and to maintain peace and unity. In Jesus' name, we pray. Amen

PEACE

Where can peace be found?
Oh where does it abound?

Is it in seclusion
Where loners withdraw
Away from the world
And all its confusion?

Is it in a bottle
Of fine port or gin,
Or is it the courts
In cases to win?

Peace can be found
Without looking all around.
It is hidden, I am told,
At the center of the soul.
It comes with a price
Given only by the Christ.

THE RETURN OF THE PRODIGAL SON

"But while the son was still a way off, his father saw him and was fill with compassion. He ran, threw his arms around his neck, and kissed him."

LUKE 15:20 KJV

When you anticipate
the return of your child, read…

GO A SECOND MILE AND MORE

"All that the Father giveth me shall come to me; and him that cometh to me I will in no wise cast out."

JOHN 6:37 KJV

Before a wild animal that has been living in captivity is reintroduced into the wild, special precautions are taken to make sure that that animal survives. What precautions are taken to make sure that prisoners cope after they have returned home from years of captivity? Are they given survival skills to adapt to the changes in their environment? Are they given a survival kit that will ensure them a new beginning? Are they monitored to see if they are adjusting to the transplant? In too many cases, I suspect, unlike with wild animals, when a prisoner is reintroduced into society, little, if anything is done to make sure that he is able to cope with his new found freedom.

Why would a newly released prisoner need survival skills and a new beginning, you may ask? The answer is simple. First, consider the changes society has made in the last 5, 10, 15, or 20 years. They are tremendous. Technology may present the greatest change with its smart phones, e-readers, and voice command computers. Trying to learn electronic gadgets by trial and errors can be daunting. A prisoner who has not experienced any of them will be lost. He may find it scary trying to transact business in banks, post offices, or other offices which require the customers to operate a computer in order to do business. No doubt his frustration and insecurity will prevent him from being successful.

Second, the financial needs of newly released prisoners are enormous. The average prisoner returns home with nothing and to nothing. He has no clothes, food, shelter, transportation, communication or any means of getting them. Worse, facing rejection after rejection, he finds that getting a job is a job in itself because many companies do not hire prisoners. What is a newly ex-con to do when has no means of livelihood? Shamefully, too many return to their old ways and soon find themselves in "revolving doors" heading back into prisons.

What can mothers do to help their children make the transition from prison back into the family and society? First, they must accept and welcome them home, being sure not to aggravate any insecurities they may have. Second, they must be understanding and patient parents. Remember, your children have been locked up like animals and as a result have developed cases of "prison mentality" – a tendency to act aggressive, defensive, submissive or unreasonable without any apparent cause. It's going to take time, understanding, and effort to rid them of it. And last, mothers must be willing to give freely of their time, possessions, and money. As I said before, most prisoners returning home have nothing. In many cases, they have lost husbands or wives and are dependent on their parents to supply their needs. When the parole board passes you the responsibility for the care of your child, accept it and be willing to go a second mile and more until your child is able to go alone.

Finally, rely on "What Would Jesus Do" to give you comfort at this jubilant but troublesome time in your life. In John 6:37 we read, "All the Father gives me shall come to me; and him that come to me, I will in no wise cast out." The implication for us is that Jesus will accept all – being careful to reject none that comes to Him regardless of the condition– into his kingdom. Just like Jesus, we should accept our children unconditionally when they are returned to us. And, just like Jesus, we should give our children provisions and protection.

Heavenly Father, stand with us as we receive our children home again. Give us the strength that we need to parent grown children whose minds have been altered by captivity. Help us to be like you – understanding, patient, and giving; and help us to go a second mild and more until our children can go alone. In Jesus' name, we pray. Amen.

A MOTHER'S PART

Many times for reasons unknown,
Some children fail to soar.
Even after they are grown,
They trip over mistake after mistake
And never rely on their own.

It is a Mother's God given part
To hold these love ones close at heart.

When you are accused of enabling, read…

RESTORE – BUT WITHHOLD SUPPORT OF DESTRUCTIVE BEHAVIORS

"I will seek the lost, bring back the strays, bandage the injured, and strengthen the weak…"

EZEKIEL 34: 16A HCSB

Enabling, the act of giving assistance to others, can be both positive and negative. It is positive when it empowers a person and allows him to continue living independently of others. On the other hand, it is negative when it cripples a person by supporting or making it easy for him to engage in destructive behaviors such as drug or alcohol abuse. There is a thin line between negative and positive enabling; making it difficult for many to tell when one stops and the other begins. Mothers of prisoners, for example, whose love for their children cause them to be quite generous, are often accused of crossing that thin line.

What are mothers to do when they are accused of enabling their children negatively? First, they must determine whether the charge if founded. Helping a child who has come home from prison with nothing is not negative enabling. In fact, it is the motherly thing to do. A good mother should make sure that she gives her child a start by providing clothing, shelter, food, and other basic needs.

After providing the basic needs, a mother should observe her child carefully. If the child is trying to get a job and trying to better himself or herself but is struggling, she should be patient and continue to assist. Under those circumstances, she is not negatively enabling. On the other hand, If your child is not making any effort to get a job or to better himself or herself, if the child sits around playing video games, or hanging with questionable friends abusing drugs or alcohol, and is constantly blaming others for his or her predicament while you take care of him or her, you have crossed the line from helping to negatively aiding your child.

Second, once you determine that you are negatively enabling your child, take steps to stop. Explain that you are going to hold him or her accountable for his or her wellbeing. If your child is staying with you, spell out to him or her the behaviors – alcohol and drug abuse, video games instead of working, etc. – that you will not tolerate and give the child time to correct them. Be sure to explain what will happen if he or she doesn't. Give an ultimatum and stick to it. If it means that you must evict your child, then do so. If your child is not staying with you but is depending on your money to survive, enforce the same rules, stop the supply of money, and practice detachment parenting —move away and let him survive on his own. It is one sure way to start him on the road to independency.

Finally, follow the Lord's example. In Ezekiel 34: 16a speaking of His beloved Israelites He said, "I will seek the lost, bring back the strays, bandage the injured and strengthen the weak…" In a nutshell, the Lord promised to restore His children on their return from captivity. Should we not do the same when our children are return to us from prison? Of course we should! But, we should be careful to aid restoration and to reframe from supporting destructive behaviors. That's what the Lord did, and that's what we should do, too.

Heavenly Father, unveil our eyes and enable us to see when we cross the line that divide positive and negative enabling. Help us to strengthen our children when they are weak, hold them accountable when they are irresponsible, and release them when they are able to go alone. In Jesus' name, we pray.
Amen

BEHOLD THY MOTHER

*Children, behold thy mother
For she is God's heavenly angel
On loan from above
An earthly vision of His agape love.*

*Her faith is unshakable
Stronger than a mighty fortress.
It is as endless as can be
Wider than the widest sea.*

*Her love is unconditional
Given completely free
Much like that of Jesus
Who lived and died for me.*

*Yes, behold thy mother.
Love and care for her
As she has cared for you.
Never ever fail to pay
Honors to her each day.*

AFTERWORD

The hold that a prison has on a person's life does not stop once the prisoner is released. The grip may continue for years, long after the sentence ends. Though the ex-convicts leave the prison with the hope of doing better, they soon find that "better" is almost impossible. For, odds are not in their favor.

First, technical schools and colleges are almost out of reach for the former prisoners. Why? Schools cost money, and the average ex-convict has no money. Also, federal grants and loans are closed to many offenders. Consequently, they cannot borrow money to get into a school. Because there are little or no job skills programs for convicts, many are left without useful life skills.

Second, most employers do not hire people with prison records. As a result, when former prisoners apply for jobs, they face rejection after rejection, even for minimum wage jobs. After a while, many soon lose hope or lose self-esteem and give up looking. They are forced to rely on the system, the family, or any means necessary for their welfare. Unless, the ex-convict can create a job – and many cannot, those means lead the person back to prison through revolving doors.

Many ex-prisoners have poor support systems. In many cases, a marriages is broken when someone is sentenced – or soon after. Therefore, most ex-convicts cannot rely on spouses. Also, family relationships are broken. For one reason or the other, families may refuse to give support, or they may not be financially able to give support. Lastly, because the economy is slow, in most towns there are little or no programs designed to help the ex-prisoner adjust to his new found freedom. In many cases, formal prisoners are left to go it alone.

No school, no jobs, and no family support: what is an ex-prisoner to do when he cannot support himself? Shamefully, too many intentionally commit crimes so that they may be sentenced to prison again. What kind of America do we live in when prison offers a better outlook for its citizens?

Finally, mothers, have you noticed that prisons spring up in or near towns with poor economic conditions? That alone is evidence that prisons are big businesses. How so, you might ask? Prisons supply hundreds of jobs, jobs supply income; subsequently, income yields profit for businesses and taxes for government. Have you also noticed who is in these prisons? The majority are blacks, the mentally ill, Mexicans or others foreigners – in other words and in some opinions, "the least of these" among us. A better question is who will create a system in which one group would profit on backs of the others? I don't know. One thing I do know is God's view is wide and His justice is sure. In His own time, He will set all things right.

As an end note, I can happily report that my son completed his sentence, managed to get a job, and has remarried. Because I know how easy it is for an ex-convict to slip back into the depth of a system which still holds him captive, I am in constant prayer for him.

ABOUT THE AUTHOR

Glory S. Davis is a retired educator with more than 40 years of experience in teaching English language arts, literature, and speech. A native of Coushatta, Louisiana, she is a graduate of Grambling State University of Grambling, Louisiana and Southeastern Louisiana University of Hammond, Louisiana. She holds a Master's Degree in Education and has held National Board Certification in English Language Arts and Literature.

A member of the United Methodist Church, she is a certified lay servant who is a key leader in the educational ministry of her church. She has served as Church school superintendent for years. In addition, she is the circuit Bible study teacher for her charge.

Since her retirement, Ms. Davis has devoted her time to writing, public speaking, and teaching Bible study. She presently resides in rural Southeastern Louisiana and is the mother of two sons.

Look for her other books– *Sometimes I Look at Sinners* and *Outside the Gates of Heaven*, which were also inspired by her Christian faith.

www.ingramcontent.com/pod-product-compliance
Lightning Source LLC
Chambersburg PA
CBHW041641090426
42736CB00034BA/3